MW00451036

WILD PERSISTENCE

Wild Persistence

POEMS

Patricia Hooper

UNIVERSITY OF TAMPA PRESS

Copyright © 2019 by Patricia Hooper. All rights reserved.

Manufactured in the United States of America
Printed on acid-free paper ∞
First Edition

On the Cover: "Homage to the Passenger Pigeon (extinct 1914)" by Suzanne Stryk
Copyright © 2019 by Suzanne Stryk. All rights reserved.
Reproduced by permission of the artist.

No part of this book may be reproduced, stored in a retrieval system, or transmit-
ted in any form or by any means, electronic, mechanical, photocopying, recording,
or otherwise, except as may be expressly permitted by the applicable copyright
statutes or in writing by the publisher.

The University of Tampa Press
401 West Kennedy Boulevard
Tampa, FL 33606

ISBN 978-159732-174-7 (hbk.)
ISBN 978-159732-175-4 (pbk.)

Browse & order online at
http://utpress.ut.edu

Library of Congress Cataloging-in-Publication Data

Names: Hooper, Patricia, 1941- author.
Title: Wild persistence : poems / Patricia Hooper.
Description: First edition. | Tampa : University of Tampa Press, [2019] |
Identifiers: LCCN 2019040153 (print) | LCCN 2019040154 (ebook) | ISBN
    9781597321747 (hardback : acid-free paper) | ISBN 9781597321754 (trade
    paperback) | ISBN 9781597321761 (ebook)
Subjects: LCGFT: Poetry.
Classification: LCC PS3558.O59 W55 2019 (print) | LCC PS3558.O59 (ebook)
    | DDC 811/.54--dc23
LC record available at https://lccn.loc.gov/2019040153
LC ebook record available at https://lccn.loc.gov/2019040154

for John

Contents

1. Sightings

2. In the Frame

3. Changing Weather

4. Next Summer's Garden

1. Sightings

Sketchbook & Journal

Dan's freezer: birds found dead along the trail
in snow ruts, autumn's crevices, the wren
almost mistaken for a leaf, the sparrow,
one red-winged blackbird lifted from a whorl
of bracken, double-bagged and zip-locked, kept
for sketching when the time comes: winter Sundays
or summer evenings on the deck, the feeders
arranged in branches overhead, above
asparagus or beans and Donna's flowers.
He isn't looking for them, but they're sometimes there—

the fledgling trapped in sleet, a finch who crashed
into the picture window, once a redstart
the cat brought home—things passing, hard to catch
in motion, dizzying till the heart has stopped.
He feeds the living, gathers up the dead
because how else to learn auriculars,
eye-rings and supercilium? How else
to come so close to seeing what they are?

Dan's essays, also: sightings, swift details
that can't be seen in flight—wild, secretive—
a voice, a look, a gesture half-perceived,
the owl's call, a quarrel with the garden,
a dying father's words . . . How to connect
these scenes until they're stilled, stalled in the heart?
They ripple from the pen and fill the page—
cold passerine, cold teal . . . cold light by which
we see the vanished life for what it was
and greet it mornings in the present world:
blue sky, gold fields, blackberries, Donna's flowers,
sun rising in the pines, and on the desk
wing-bars and stripes, the margins of a feather—
what the mind salvages to study later.

The Copperhead

Coiled like a vine along the lower wall,
it seemed to *be* the vine: then it moved a little,
its orange head lifted, body a rope of silk,
the hourglass bands around it like a bracelet.
I stepped back for the shovel. When I thrust
it down, the viper slid—the thinnest sound—
straight for my leg. But first it hesitated

*

not long enough to see the rim of trees,
to see the houses leaning toward the hills,
to see the hills far off, the grey-blue mountain,
to see the pink crape myrtle in the yard,
to see the front porch with its pail of berries,
to see my knees, blue-stained from berry picking,
to see the bare skin shining at my ankle,
to see, if it sees at all, the chance before it,
to see what I might see for the last time
if no one came, if I was among the few
for whom its venom is a lethal poison.

*

And then whatever it saw or didn't see
of the world and plunging blade was stopped forever.
I left it for the birds. And the birds came,
the black ones, circling, mantling in the shade.
The day went on just as it had beforehand
except for a quiver under every leaf
and grass blade, something silent, slithering, driven
by danger or revenge. For they must have *known*.
But there was the garter snake curled on the sidewalk,
sunning, the way a baby takes a nap

on a blanket at a picnic, undisturbed
by voices, singing, even an argument,
or the sun's passage over the summer garden,
whatever's come and gone.

Sudden

Early morning, the first
flight of the day, and I've had
my ticket for less than an hour,
so I'm hardly surprised when the guard
asks me to step aside
and goes through my carry-on bag
and my purse and my pockets. Oh
yes, this journey is sudden:
my daughter has called in the night
and her husband is dead, and her children,
so little, are just waking up
to no father, and soon she will tell them.
Sudden. And now it is daylight,
the sun's coming up, igniting
the towers and tarmac, the plane's
at the gate, the passengers boarding,
and although I am told I can go
I stand there uncertain. I know
that someone is slipping a blade
in his laptop or lining his shoes
with explosives or planting a bomb
in the cabin, it's going to be
sudden, no guard can detect it,
nothing's secure.

Moving South

1.

You're back again, bright bird who often came
when I emptied out the coffee grounds among
the annuals and the worms came up, red breast
beside the pink impatiens. After a year
of seeing nothing, doing almost nothing
apart from moving in, I step outside,
still homesick, far from home, and you appear:
you're splashing in the puddles, pulling up
the worms. Bird of my own
lost garden, what are you doing here?

2.

Last winter as we unpacked a cardinal
sat for a moment in the pines. I thought
he might have come from home where snow was falling
the afternoon we left. Then I remembered:
they take the frozen seeds, the icy berries—
they never have to leave. He wasn't ours.

3.

Not one but several. Always in a pair
or pair of pairs, the goldfinches are back
to match the yellow rose, the gold lantanas.
I almost lose them when they pass the sunflowers.
Wild, fluttering petals? No, they've reached the feeder.

4.

And something else: the slender mockingbird
whose melodies astound me, flash of grey
and white in the pink crape myrtle near the porch.
Midsummer, and the tree is blossoming
and nearly faded now. I hadn't looked.

5.
Late afternoon: a gust, descending wings.
I've seen you in the snow but not in summer
stalking the chipmunks, sending the finches flying.
So you've arrived at last, or were you here,
waiting, until a joy, a rare abundance
should overtake the garden? Then you fall
over the finch's nest. I should have known.

6.
And in the woods this morning a commotion
of colors—orange, black, white. An oriole lights
on the willow oak, then on the broken fountain.
Bold, bright, conspicuous, quick—it has to be.
Almost before I see it, it disappears.

7.
A hummingbird—oh, a tiny, tiny thing!
I have to squint to see it. Didn't you say,
when I was staring over the precipice,
focus on something small . . .

8.
They've found the fountain, stone boy, curly-haired,
riding a dolphin from whose mouth the water
spills to the clamshell pool: two cedar wax-wings
splashing the purple phlox, the blue verbenas.
And on the ground, alone, the mourning dove,
color of rain and shadow, voice of sorrow
among the lighter notes. An undertone.

9.

Bluebird, building again in the same house
you found in spring, you have to fly across
my yard to get there, then to my neighbor's pines
and down to your nesting box above the roses.
You never crossed my path in Michigan,
but here you are, a new and busy brightness,
diligent in your work. They say you come
three times, if you come at all, although each brood
will be a little smaller, and next summer
you may not come again. Today you clear
your old nest from the box as if you're planning
to build another. Maybe you'll settle in.

Here, in the Piedmont

In Gastonia the downtown's boarded up
except for Ford's where you can still buy
seeds by the ounce from Mason jars or ask for
"thirty feet of cantaloupes" or "a hill of beans,"

and the antique shop with its rusty iron tables,
trendy for patios, and wicker planters
that need re-weaving like those three cane chairs

I saw this morning sitting in the rain—
someone will make them right—and Tony's Ice Cream,
quiet in early March, and the local hardware
no longer, as the sign says, *Fully Stocked . . .*

But back to Ford's: birdfeeders by the dozens
and whirligigs and bright blue gardening gloves
and flats of pansies. If your job at the mill is gone,

if you worked for forty years in the one that closed
in Clover, you could plant a pack of seeds,
pumpkins or melons, peas or Indian corn,
and sell them at the market. You could buy a sack

of onion sets for fifty cents. And even
if you had no place to plant, you could stand outside
among the bags of mulch and talk to neighbors

about the price of gas and which tomatoes
do well in pots and where the fish are biting.
You could pass the time and see how folks are coping
till something at the new Walmart opens up.

Elegy for a Son-in-law

1.

A distant figure on the mountainside
seems to be coming closer, then it turns,
a blue, retreating cap, a scarlet jacket.
Without another sign, I know you're there,
climbing again the way you used to climb
before you were a ghost. I want to call
Don't go! Come back! I have your two small sons
sleeping behind me in the car, their mother
watching the sky for falcons. But you move
farther away. Or we do. Now you're gone,
back toward Mount Sterling where she took your ashes.
I hope it's peaceful there. I hope you know
they're doing well. I hope you didn't see us.

2.

These are the mountains where you were a boy,
broad waves of mountains rolling like an ocean
into the distance, no horizon, only
these smoky contours where you knew each rise
and hemlock forest, plunging stream. Your friends
tell how you often left them for a while
after you'd reached the top, to be alone,
then met them at the camp, all tales and laughter.
Today, a red-tailed hawk riding the breeze,
gold leaves, cascading creeks—your kind of joy:
cold, rushing currents, then the ecstatic slide.

3.

This is the world you wanted: brisk fall air,
the valleys hung with haze, that long blue range
half-hidden by the clouds. It's coming clear.
How far you must have seen from there! And here?
It's hard to see around so many hills,

so many peaks and gorges, and the curves
are slippery on the parkway, miles of turns.
We're heading home. The boys are waking now,
their mother's passing crackers, pointing out
the overlook ahead: blue waterfall,
deep river valley, autumn leaves, the pines
along the ridge, the rising trail—and there,
the summit you'd have shown them. Mist and shine.

The Spider

Summer is almost gone. I noticed it
when I went to fill the feeder: chrysanthemums
wearing a hint of gold, though they won't steal
the whole show till September.

                              And for now
August luxuriates: blowsy
overblown roses heavy as hydrangeas, waves
of purple Russian sage, and a whole chorus
of yellow-throated trumpet lilies. Yes, let's have it—
extravagance at the end!

Something is missing though: the fat brown spider
I stepped on near the porch last night, its web
large as a dinner platter at the door.
Soon afterward I heard the rain begin,
and now, today, only the empty web
remains, tattered but glistening . . .

It's strange, something dies
and the world stays: breezes, an iridescent beetle
creeping up the rose stems, and the sun
warm on the metal sprinkling can. And somewhere
far away, the ripples I used to see
in childhood at the lake. September came,
we'd pack the car for home, and school would start,
and sometimes, sitting at my desk, I'd see
the dock, the sand's hard ridges, and the waves
still there without me, lapping at the shore.

Fall Changes

I left those three crows
the last corn in my garden,
and not one thanked me.

*

Bright August sunlight
but just north of the woodpile
a November wind.

*

September begins
with a vee of geese flying
and two fat, slow frogs.

*

All night fallen leaves
pile up under the maples—
old thoughts, cast away.

*

A ragged black glove
high in the oak's bare branches
flies away, cawing.

*

Through the leafless hedge
a neighbor I've never met
waves from her window.

Evening at a Mountain Inn

Dinner arrives at seven
in deep, triangular dishes meant to fit
the giant lazy Susan: country ham,
fried chicken, mashed potatoes, black-eyed peas,
biscuits and gravy, collards, grits with cheese,
and okra fritters, just to name a few
of the evening's offerings. Our innkeeper,
a Southern Baptist in flannel shirt and jeans,
prays heartily as all the guests join hands,

though few of us have met: two stylish matrons
up for the night from Charlotte, a fisherman
eager to try the streams, and a young lawyer
with his bride of seven weeks. They're here to hike
before boar season complicates the scene
or snow descends. After a day outdoors
everyone has a tale to tell, a creek
or trail to recommend. But first, as our first-
grade teacher from the Outer Banks reminds us,
everyone's *starving* . . .

          The lazy Susan spins,
and after the coffee and the pumpkin pie
we step outside. The front porch is complete
with rockers, though the view at six thousand feet
has almost disappeared, a few pink stains
streaking the sky along the western rim.
Are we obliged to speak? But someone's brought
his dulcimer and begins to strum. A breeze
rises in the upper branches of the pines,
and everyone's quiet, listening, lost in thought.
Night seeps up from the valley. And even with

your hand in mine, I'm floating, drifting out
like smoke from the chimney, comfortably alone
in the communal dark.

Apple

The apple floats with the moon
over the orchard. Darkness

has hidden the trees and left it
adrift on the air where the moon

finds it and lights it. Golden
Delicious and drab by day,

now it tosses among the clouds
like a ball cast into orbit,

a planet riding the sparks
of Orion's heel. Soon,

caught by the wind, it will fall
to the floors of the earth, but for now

it is sailing a shoreless ocean,
white-capped and starry. All day

the wagons rolled through the orchard
bearing bushels of apples, red

and gold plucked from their moorings
and carried away. Tonight

on the seas of the sky, one apple
remains, rising and falling,

free of the harvest, its cargo
the first crisp snowfall

of winter, a ballast
of black seeds safe in its hold.

My Junco

This morning another wild flight
interrupted:

the Dark-eyed Junco
hitting the picture window—

no, he was dead, not stunned.

And how elegant he was
when I lifted him

from the patio—
slate feathers and soft, grey throat.

And how perfectly he fit
the palm of my gardening glove

as I wrapped him in oak leaves
and buried him in the earth.

Another of the world's
beautiful ideas
lost,

but nourishing the next one—

those Whirlwind anemones
I planted under the oak tree

beside him—
next summer's wings.

August in the Little Field

Have you ever heard
of a purpose as clear
as this one:

the goldfinch
alight on the lavender thistle?

All morning
she's been stripping the seeds, flying
from her nest to the nodding blossom.

And hasn't she waited
since April for it to bloom?

Now it is time, high summer—

yet how many others
do you know with such resolute
patience?

Maybe the monarch
searching for milkweed, maybe

the cabbage moth looking for cabbage.
But I hardly know anyone

anymore who lives like the goldfinch,
who knows that whatever
she needs will arrive in time.

All spring she flew back and forth
over the meadow, watching,

while the sparrows were nesting, the robins
were feeding their young.

The warm season wore on—

and then, in mid-summer, the seeds
she would feed her nestlings.

Wasn't it wisdom
not to have given up?

All morning I've thought,
suppose she had doubted, suppose
she'd grown tired of waiting?

But I think she knew better
of the fields and their bright design,

and the ways of the rain,
and the shifts in the light,
in the weather,

her faith so simple
I could only wish it were mine.

2. In the Frame

In the Clearing

After last night's rain the woods
smell sensual—a mixture of leaves and musk.
The morels have disappeared, and soon I'll come across
those yellow chanterelles, the kind they sell
in town at the farmers' market. Once I saw
the Swedish woman who raises her own food
foraging for them, two blond boys
quarrelling near the pickup, and the next morning
they were selling them from their stand beside the road.

Out here, among last year's dead
leaves with the new shoots of spruces
poking through them, I've come to the place where light
brightens a glade of ferns and the log someone else
placed here—carved *B. W.*—where I sometimes sit
to listen to the birds. Today the sun is breaking through
the wet branches, revealing a clean sky,
brilliant, cerulean. Then, suddenly, a raft of scudding clouds

promising more rain. If it comes, I'll read all afternoon—
Henry James, or maybe Eudora Welty's
Delta Wedding, where so many characters
vie for attention I can never keep them straight.
Here, there's no one else, no one to worry over
or argue with or love. Maybe the earth was meant
only for this: small comings and goings
on the forest floor, the understory astir
with its own secret life. If I sit still enough
among the damp trees, sometimes I see the world
without myself in it, and—it always surprises me—
nothing at all is lost.

One Day

The mockingbird sings
every morning at seven
in seven voices.

*

If only I had
nothing to do all summer
but admire the birds.

*

Then something goes dark—
the blinds closing next door in
all the bright windows.

*

It must have been then
that my friend's son was placing
the gun in his mouth.

*

His mother comes home,
enters the kitchen, calling.
Who can love the world?

*

Did the birds notice
that hole in the blue daylight
a finch might pass through?

*

Friends stand on her porch
a long time as if daring
themselves to enter.

*

And the mockingbird,
without manners or mercy,
sings from her rooftop.

Sunflowers

Whenever I drive west
to the farmers' market, I see the mountain
rising beyond the highway, and I think again
of the three-year-old last summer, falling
from the cliff. His father
had turned away only for a moment
and then looked back—the sunny path was empty.

And down below who knows
what he saw first: a blue jacket?
a blond head? Or maybe just the kudzu
taking over. There was no one to call
out to or send for help. Finally a ranger
spotted the father clambering down the rocks
but reached the boy too late.

Now it's fall again, and the car radio
brings news of another bombing
in Iraq. I see it in immediate
detail: the cheerful crowds
of shoppers and busy vendors, bright displays
of vegetables and fruit. Then
mayhem: a car rigged with explosives
rolling toward them,
the bodies of the blameless
ripped apart.

At the farmers' market I buy plums,
acorn squash and melons and,
to feed the birds, two huge, stemless
sunflowers, maybe the very ones
I saw last summer in a farmhouse yard, so tall
by July they seemed almost human. Now they lie

on the front seat beside me, enormous
halos of ochre petals, their seed-packed heads
lopped off . . .
Once they lived
their whole lives in a garden, and all day,
every day, they turned their faces slowly
from east to west, as if their one purpose
was to grow sunward, following the sun.

Paris

I'm thinking tonight of Paris,
of the woman trapped in the street
when the terrorist's gun jammed,
how she ran for her life in the seconds
he took to reload. Isn't this
how nightmares usually end:
the bomb fails to explode,
and we wake safe in our beds,
alive and well after all?

But I'm thinking, too, of the girl
at the concert who heard gunshots
and thought they were sound effects,
then watched as the rifles fired
and her friends fell, one by one.
Didn't she think they would live?
Life always goes on, doesn't it,
when you're twenty-five?

               When she felt
the bullet lodge in her chest,
didn't she think she'd be spared
by some miracle still to come,
something she searched in vain for
with her already sightless eyes?

In the Frame

Looking out through a narrow pane
of glass in the larger window
I saw how the scene came closer
like the ones Van Gogh isolated
in his perspective frame.
The view, as he wrote, was foreshortened
by borders, the single haystack
no longer lost in the greater
expanse of the summer field.
What I saw was the trumpet lily
without the surrounding garden,
without the competing figures
in the foreground, those phlox and asters
that made it seem so far.
The white lily moved toward me
the way when the surgeon held
your x-ray against the light
he blocked its peripheral features
with both hands, setting apart
what became the entire picture,
making me look
where I had to now, at the heart.

A Wake of Vultures

Black as the night that has lifted
they are here as I pass the lake
this morning, twenty or thirty
convening along the banks
or standing hunch-shouldered in trees,
bald clerics greeting each other,
a convocation of birds.

On other mornings I've noticed
only a heron fishing
or a flock of egrets dissolving
into the mist where the lake
undulates in the sunlight,
reflecting the cypresses,
white wings or a drift of clouds.
Today it is blank, steel grey
and motionless, and the air
reeks of decay, of carcasses
drained and devoured, and among them,

this milling of somber judges
decked out in their long, stark robes,
these undertakers awaiting
a new day and its work.
They have found me, these dark angels
I had thought to escape. And now,
all at once, they are off

in a maelstrom of wing beats, destroying
the blue silence of dawn.
A grave darkness has flown
leaving the shoreline empty

of dying, the thought of dying,
clearing the world of its endings,
its litter of scraps and rags.

The Missing Girl

Every morning I pass the photo
of the missing girl. There she is, on the billboard
north of the interstate: light brown hair
cut short, eyes grey—or is it the mist
rising off the river, which they dredged twice
last fall, trying to find her. In the picture she's
about seven—a school photo—and she's smiling in her plaid
uniform with the round, white collar. Someone saw
her backpack and her school books
in the park, someone found her sweater on a low branch
near the woods. For a long time
police and neighbors kept searching, and every night
her parents on the late news pleading, *Please,
please, she needs her inhaler* . . . Then it was
winter: ice on the lake and river, nights below
zero, deep snow. Every morning when I drove past
she looked colder, shivering in her short sleeves, icicles
dangling from the broken light fixture just above
her head. Once in a snow squall I couldn't
see her at all, she was nowhere, but the next week
it was April, birds were building a big nest
where the icicles had melted, and the top right
corner of the photograph had peeled off
a little, taking some of her hair and clothes. Sometimes
in the spring rains she seemed nearly transparent,
and all summer the sun kept bleaching her pale face
paler. Now it's fall again, the nest has blown
away, and school has started. She'd be in a new
class by now, with a new teacher and a new desk, one
of those girls I saw yesterday in the drugstore, shopping
for notebooks and broad, bright crayons. I could almost
see her there among them, adding candy to her basket
at the checkout, but this morning when I look up, she's
still here, waiting beside the highway, growing older.

From a Park Bench

Under the green domes of maples
light spangles the abundant slabs of moss.
Grass won't grow here, but something else has taken
over. When I went into the drugstore yesterday
the clerk who moved away had been replaced

by a girl who looked so much like her
I thought for a moment she'd come back to town
with her hair cut. And in the second grade,
when Bobby Markley died, a new boy from Ohio
promptly sat beside me at his desk.

Out here, in the city park,
people are almost always interchangeable,
though the summer I'll hate to lose
supplants itself with a wan and amber sun
that isn't quite the same, reminding me

of larger griefs not easily consoled.
"Life is the saddest thing there is,
next to death," Edith Wharton wrote,
she who walked so often in the park
listening to the old, remembered voices.

She must have sat under trees not unlike this one,
heavy with sorrows she couldn't speak aloud.
She mourned her friends, and "one friend like no other,"
while the late sunlight passed across the grasses,
and now she too is gone.

Lakewood Path

The woman and the man taking a walk
stop for a moment, as if noticing,
suddenly, where they are. It is a park,
a mulched path through the woods of ash and oak
and maples tinged with orange and gold: September
beginning as summer closes its last act.
Maybe the aging heart can play it better

than the starlet with her flowery boas, cloudless
blue scarves and grassy skirts. The woman
walking beside her friend could tell you this
and gauge the coming weather: three weeks more
of brilliant skies and gardens—dahlias, asters—
and then the soft descent for which the birds
are swarming, readying in the highest boughs.
They know it's almost over, time to go—

what didn't happen earlier won't happen.
But the man pauses, looking toward the lake.
What was it, years ago, that made her startle,
seeing him staring so? They share a past,
such as it is, and small: they've both been lost
for long, long moments in those dazzling waters,
hardly enough to set the stage, and yet

the stage is set. She has only to touch his sleeve
or he, her shoulder. After so many years,
instead, they watch one silver boat, far out,
in which—but who knows what is going on
so far from shore?—two people sit, two vague
and minor characters. Or are these our actors,
an imagined future the plot is hurrying toward?
But the boat seems ever smaller, disappearing,
and now the sun's rays, blinding, block it out

as the day drops farther down the blond horizon
until, at last, the only thing that's certain
is the sense of a curtain slowly coming down.

Autumn

This is the season
when the soul begins setting out
from the body, the way leaves
tug at the elm's branches,
beginning to let go
of summer, practicing
for that last skittery dance
into oblivion. Walking
home under burnished trees,
I button my coat collar
tighter against the chill
as one day I'll try to keep
the soul wrapped in the body's
comfort, forgetting the lesson
of leaves. Look, even now,
how vibrant they're all
becoming, escaping the black
cages of branches, floating
free for the first time, flaunting
their golds, crimsons and ochres,
and how could we call it dying,
this flying, the way they're rising
light as the sparks of bonfires,
igniting the whole boulevard,
twisting and turning themselves
into wings of flame.

A Death in Winter

It was over. I had done
what I could do. Now
I walked among the bare trees
wanting nothing. Or,
as I came to understand,
oblivion. It was the frozen
landscape that took me in, the white arms
of the garden, flowers
absent or asleep. The sky
colorless. Like looking in a mirror,
I suppose. And then,
weeks, months later that decisive
hand touching the universe: pear,
hawthorn, magnolia, dogwood
and, beneath them,
daffodils, the scilla's
cobalt bells. How pitiful
it was, the world resigned
to loss, but fickle,
fickle. All it took
was one gesture. Then the trees
abandoning their vows, the tulips
sensual, outrageous. What
appalled me was betrayal: one breeze
over the planet, then spring's
masterful seductions and the leaves
gone dizzy with excitement. One
touch. Yes, even
for a brief, unthinking moment,
my response.

Sandhill Cranes

One morning in Sarasota
    two cranes came to my door.

They walked right up to my window
    in their scarlet caps,

and the tallest, who saw his reflection,
    began dancing,

his wings, six feet across,
    rose in the air

as he leapt in his black leather slippers,
    his coat of feathers,

and pranced like an Iroquois brave
    to impress his bride.

But his rival, all glassy shimmer,
    was pirouetting

in the room with its leafy sofa
    and flowered chairs.

Oh I know what they say in legends,
    and no wonder:

if a crane lands on your roof
    someone will die,

if a crane flies through your house
    you will live forever.

But who knows what it means when they stroll
    straight to your window,

bowing and strutting again,
    though they mate for life?

I only know this: I thought it was fine
    and lucky

that they came to visit,
    I thought it was just in time

that they found their way to the house
    in which I was grieving,

and the weights flew from my shoulders
    seeing them rise

and disappear
    into the sunny morning

where I stood staring up long after
    in my surprise.

3. Changing Weather

Early Morning, After Snow

I woke at 4 a.m. to the sound
of a plow struggling up the road—
a deep snow must have fallen.

And the room was almost bright
the way it is when moonlight
shines on ice. I heard
what seemed to be the plow
turning around

and giving up on *us*. There'd be
no newspaper, no mail . . .
I could have gone back to sleep,

but instead I watched the moon
grow fainter in the gradually
lightening sky. It seemed
to be floating in a snow-clogged stream,

and the stars, too, were floating,
dim sediments that sank into the depths
like thoughts without conclusions,

dense, cool, and alluvial.

In the Butterfly Aviary

January: the glare
   of ice over grey roads,
but inside this
   steamy terrarium
     everything's heated up

to a steady eighty. Even
   the guard's in his element,
vacationing for the day
   in Brazil, or leading a tour
     through an Amazon rain forest.

When the Blue Morpho alights
   on his cap, he announces, "The largest
butterfly in the house,"
   to the schoolchildren who catch
     on their shoulders the smaller parcels,

checkerspots, admirals,
   and the rare Archduke, for which
the guard summons his reverence.
   It might well be a circus,
     those two metalmarks perched

on the teacher's hair, or the sulphur
   chasing a red-cheeked girl,
but the guard ushers the class
   to a chrysalis in the corner
     where rebirth is the lesson.

Brief lesson! It's kindergarten,
   so he isn't surprised when the children
move on to the Atlas Moth

spread flat on the oleander.
    They'd like to stretch out like that

in the heat and give up their loads
    of snowsuits and strings of mittens,
which they drop, just thinking it, under
    a blizzard of Blue-winged Hairstreaks
      from Costa Rica. No,

it isn't these fancy imports
    who've stolen the show, but simply
the pool under the fountain,
    which the children are drifting toward
      with the tigerwings, sprawling out

on the moss-covered brink where a boy
    opens his palm and produces
a pebble, letting it slip
    overboard in an instant.
      For a moment the morning's quiet

as they lie watching the leaves
    reflected in ripples, stirring
the warm bath with their fingers,
    swallowtails on their backs,
      which they hardly notice, as if

the sky weren't glass and that ledge
    of snow hung on the leaded
bars holding it up
    were only a cloud passing over
      their hands dipped in the mirror

everything's tumbled under:
  trees, vines, butterflies, sky,
and the guard's wavery face
  staring back with their own from a place
  they'd almost forgotten, summer.

February Thaw

Out of the mist—or is it
out of a melting drift—

this trowel reappears,
cast off, it seems—last summer's

abandoned resolution.
Or was there an early snowstorm

that sent its owner rushing
indoors, forgetting something?

Like a thought that re-emerges
months afterward, just where

the mind left off, this trowel,
hot pink with a lime-green handle,

leans upright against a porch
I pass on my morning walk,

a relic from the past,
and not what I first guessed

from a block away, the earliest
hyacinth of the season.

Winter Move

The van had pulled away
from the curb an hour ago,
and I was the last one out.
I checked the kitchen faucet—no leak—
and adjusted the thermostat.
It was cold in the house, too cold

in the entry where all day
the movers had been hurrying through the door,
wrestling chairs and tables and the heavy boxes
I'd packed with everything I thought I'd want—
including Grandma's china, which in thirty years
I'd hardly ever used.

                    By afternoon
the rain that fell at lunch time turned to snow,
faintly at first, but now it was coming down
in large, erratic flakes, collecting on
the kitchen window panes. On winter days,
watching the snow accumulate, I'd plan
next summer's garden while I dried the plates.
Now someone else would rake away the mulch.

And even indoors there was nothing left to do
except to go upstairs and check the closets
for something left behind. But there was nothing—
nothing to show where the children kept their trophies
or baseball cards or dolls, or where they slept.
And then I saw our empty room, the carpet
with its deep prints from our bed.

You tapped the horn—
the car was ready—and by now the van

must be on the interstate. When I'd locked the door,
our dear, finicky lock, I pressed the key
into my palm until it left a mark,
then dropped it through the mail slot. I could hear it
chime on the floor below . . .
                              As we drove away,
streetlights were coming on, and snow was falling
so thickly that my footprints and the ruts
left by the van had already filled with snow.

Spring Sequence

A white hen
rushes behind the hen house—
winter, hurrying off.

*

Ice melts in the grass, a woman
laughing, undoing buttons.
Tonight, lying awake,
I hear how the pond hardens
again, north of the boulder.

*

Crocuses in the lawn
where I didn't plant them!
A chipmunk, a squirrel buried
these flags—purple and yellow—
making me mow in zig-zags,
changing my wet, dark path.

*

No leaves on the branches, yet
I wake, thinking I hear them
in the sudden rainfall.

*

The pear blooms and the dogwood,
two girls in their white dresses.
When they change quietly
into their green street clothes,
I stand squinting to see them
as they vanish into a crowd.

All Morning

The mockingbird this morning in the oak
was tripping off its medley as the sun rose,
a repertoire of cardinals, finches, jays.
Sometimes we only need the imitation,
the skillful repetition of the real
to give us back the world.

                It sang its heart out,
and sometimes something in the woods beyond it
would answer in its only native song,
a limited and artless string of notes.
We hear it, and we know what will appear:
red-winged, buff-crested, black-tailed, yellow-feathered,
among the summer leaves.

                But a mockingbird
is clever, like a crow, and though it doesn't
count or tease the owls, it improvises
and steals what it admires, and at times
it strikes what seems a new, surprising tune,
something the singer hasn't quite expected,
arranged in ways the world has never heard.
All morning flickers, warblers, evening grosbeaks
sang from the woods, and I was glad to hear them,
though when I looked above me in the branches,
I saw one bird.

End of Summer in the Piedmont

At last the hot and humid air gives way
to a chill morning—not
in August, as it sometimes does up north,

but by October most of the summer birds
have vanished, and the leaves begin to show
their transitory colors: red and gold
travelling down King's Mountain. In another month
my neighbors who leave each weekend for the shore
will think of staying home.

And I'll wash the downstairs windows, mow the lawn,
which leaps to grow again, invigorated
by the cooler days and nights. All summer, hot—
defeated by the heat—I'd go outside
only when necessary, and while my friends
in Michigan were jogging into town

or playing tennis in the park, I'd sit
on the stifling porch and think of heroines
in southern plays or novels: sultry, steamy
women whose ways I didn't understand
before—like Blanche du Bois reclining in a chair,
restless, desirous, half-daft, but barely able
to rise, or lift a hand . . .

Path

A wet fall morning,
burnished leaves stuck to the path
like bronze cobblestones

leading to the edge
of the ravine. Someone's made
a sign, *Nature Trail,*

and a white birch log
marks where it begins. Then you're
out there on your own

like the fox, rabbit,
and raccoon. Today an owl
flies over Clark's Pond

heading for the creek.
On the way, deer tracks, candy
wrappers, two beer cans,

remains of a fire.
The woods are already bare
except for the nests

and those five black birds
crossing a grey sky, making
one line of haiku.

October Garden

Today I have read the news
of men lopping off heads
as if they were slicing the stalks
of lilies, and I have heard
how the mind retains consciousness
for seconds after the stroke.

And because it is time
to cut back the fall garden
with its scent of death,
this morning I raked asters
and phlox onto the compost
and saw not flowers and stems
but bodies tossed into graves.

This garden knows nothing of terror.
Its season has ended, and next year
it will have other lives.
Beside me a basket of bulbs
waits to be planted, and somewhere
someone not thinking of flowers
is sharpening knives.

Circling O'Hare

October. Early dark. An emptiness
above, below, in which we're biding time
until the runway clears, the evening storms

moving across the skyline. Now the lamps
are coming on, the necklaces of headlights
along the interstates and avenues,
and overhead, the stars.

                    Our cabin's lit,
a capsule in the ranging darknesses,
as if we're stalled somewhere between the earth
and nothing.

            Down below, invisible,
waiting to meet me in the parking lot,
my son is on his phone, checking arrivals
or calling home to say that we'll be late.
It must be raining there, a gentle rain,
the thunder easing, slowly moving off . . .

Only the thought of rain and someone waiting
convinces me I'm tethered to the world.

December: in the South

The year's first Christmas cards arrived
just as camellias opened near
the mailbox—hot pink
blossoms I had never seen
up north. They bloomed

profusely, the way my fuchsia roses bloomed
in Michigan last summer. I was
suddenly sick for home

and my sunny window just above the sink
that looked out on the garden. Today
would be bright and cold, a thin snow
falling on the drifts, cardinals
vying for the feeders. I could almost hear
the plow as it groaned and struggled
up the road . . .

          And the new owners,
a couple with a baby, might be stamping
their boots at the back door, or maybe he
was away for the day at work, and she
was hanging the new curtains
or standing in the kitchen
stirring soup . . .

          When I opened up
the mailbox, absently, I saw a square
white envelope from home, and found myself
pressing it to my face, as if it carried
snow, or the scent of snow . . .

4. Next Summer's Garden

Driving North

A doe steps from the woods,
coaxing a fawn so new
its legs collapse on pavement.

You swerve to change your path,
hoping to hear no other
approaching car for miles,
no other traveler

in the early summer evening.
Behind, in the rearview mirror,
dusk settles in, the fawn
still struggling to stand

on the rain-slick rim of chance.
There's nothing you can do,
no way to reach them there
in the other kingdom.

And when the headlights come,
as you knew they must, you pray
into the wilderness
that enough time is left

for things to right themselves
again. The sky is clear.
You roll the window down
to hear what news there is:

the rushing summer leaves,
the passing tires.

Auguries

Disturbances of air, those flocking birds
that leaf the sugar maple in the yard
in late October after the leaves have fallen.
On the porch today I thought, abstracted, *summer*,
but then they lifted, almost all at once,
leaving the maple bare. Later a crow,
hectoring what may have been an owl
in the branches of the pines.

                         Two months ago,
when my daughter called, an intermittent static
kept breaking up her voice . . . *an accident* . . .
air-lifted . . . *spinal cord* . . . *paralysis* . . .
her seven-year-old who couldn't feel his legs.
It was an August evening, clear and warm,
and through the open window I could hear
a wood thrush, warbling . . .

                         It must have been
terror that made me fasten on the least
bright harbingers of hope: small, singing birds,
a summer evening's calm. But as I drove
to the airport, on the highway, there they were,
a flock of crows descending on the limping
jay along the shoulder, closing in
before they touched the ground. And for a moment
I saw them from below, as the jay saw them,
blocking the sun, a blackness at the center,
wings sucking the light out of the air.

Prognosis

Some things the mind
cannot take in

entirely, as if
to spare itself

or let the sense
seep in

over a month,
a year.

Reason absorbs
one drop, and then

the next
of what might be a flood

too great to bear.
A dam could break.

Some things the mind
keeps from itself

unknowingly. It knows
what it can take.

Lens

How different things must have looked
to my mother than they did to me.
There I am in the black-and-white photo
the summer the baby died.
I'm seven, trying out my pogo stick
with the two new girls next door.
We're laughing, and I'm shouting something
to my brother, who wants his turn.
And there's Dad, standing near the station wagon,
staring at the grass.
She must have stood far back, under the pear tree,
focusing, trying to fit us in.

After

After I left your body to be burned;
after I drove off
into the morning of maples and elms and oaks
tossing their brilliant cargoes to the ground;
after I drove back
for your sweater, your reading glasses, and the vase of flowers;
after I gave you up
to the minister and the mourners and the busy church
and the newspapers where I would place your name
and the names of the new survivors; after I came
to the graves where your parents lay under moss and stones;
after I let you go
to the grasses, the falling leaves, and the coming winter;
after I came home
to my house in another city and the evening rain
and unpacked the boxes and placed your things with my things,
your clock already on time here, your shining face
in the photograph, and your afghan in which I wrapped
myself as if in your arms; after I slept
and woke; after I saw you as if you sat
in the room, as you often had; after I knew
what to do with myself, I began sorting your books,
your beloved novels, their pages worn by your hands,
and picked up your knitting and saw how in time I could start
the last sleeve and finish it as you had planned,
and unpacked your dishes, setting the flowered plates
on the blue table cloth, just as you always had,
although I stood at a great height looking down
at the room and myself in it; after I saw
how far I had followed you, farther than you would have asked,
I saw I was looking back from the other world.

Little Brothers

My little brothers,
nobody brought you home
from the hospital. Twice
our father set up the crib.
There was a soft, square blanket
and a moon overhead with a key
to sing you to sleep. I never
saw it again. I wondered
for years what the song was.

*

Once, in the night, I heard whining
It was the neighbor's cat,
restless in heat. I was glad
when I looked in at my mother
asleep, hearing no one crying
at the door of the dark house.

*

Fifty years later I sit
through the long days of her dying,
wanting to keep her with me.
When I touch her hair,
sometimes I feel you waking
in your coracles in the rushes
on the other shore.

Next Summer's Garden

The ruffled, flamboyant blooms
of the Dutch-blue irises
sway in the morning air. I planted them
last summer, unaware
of how sick my mother was
and that she wouldn't see
another spring.

June now. I'm setting in
pink peonies to join them, and the early gold
daylily, *lilioasphodelus*, the one
Aristotle may have noticed
in his garden. How he must have loved
being paid to classify
the plants and meadow spiders! He was proof
that nature's pleasures fuel philosophy.

And my mother would have liked
these newcomers among the crowds
of roses—Lady Wenlock,
Miss Alice, Constance Spry—their common names
like the names of characters in the nineteenth-century
novels she loved to read. Like Fanny Price
at Mansfield Park, they may not
bloom well for another year,

and who knows what
will have taken place by then? Some
heaved by the frost, others overtaken
by weeds or by disease . . .

Sometimes I hear her saying
Don't overdo or just my name
from somewhere near the ash tree,

but it's only grief
trying to fill up space,

or my imagination
of which she always said
I had too much.

Just yesterday
I thought she touched me on
my shoulder when I bent to start
the mower, as if she still
frets over me, worries to see me grieve.

Steps

At ninety-five my father takes the steps,
gripping the wooden post, the iron railing,
no longer the fellow who used to sprint upstairs
at seventy. To get to the restaurant

takes time and patience and a degree of balance
he doesn't trust he has. I walk behind
in case he falls my way, surprised to see
how tightly he grasps, with unreliable fingers,
the barely steadying structures of the world.

Sightings

The world leafs out again, the willows first
and then the river birches near the road
we're driving down, you in your car seat watching
for hawks or smaller birds, returning home.
Two years have passed since you could walk or stand
alone. The winter-damaged fields are sown,
and there, along the ridge, unraveling,
spirals of song birds, drifts of dogwood trees
restored to blossom, beauty that breaks the heart.
And you whose spinal cord could not be healed:
you're lowering the window, looking up
at miles of wings, your face alive with joy.

In Tennessee

The Blue Ridge at sunset—hardly a missed note
in the hemlocks where a mockingbird is singing
while to the west a falcon dips, then glides
over the valley, indistinct from here
except that the bird falls lower than the chair
I'm sitting in, and disappears. The sky
is the color of pomegranate, and the balcony
slips into shadow like the distant hills.
No wonder that the mockingbird is singing
a medley of every song he knows,
no matter whose. No wonder that he sits
in the glow of a single flood lamp high above
the roof, a pool he must mistake for sunlight,
enough to urge him on and on and through
his repertoire that bird by bird is ringing
over the day's end, over the night's coming.
Maybe he has to sing to know himself
as part of things—finch, cardinal, wren, and now
that long, coarse call that sounded like the crow
or Steller's jay—whatever voice he's pulling
out of himself, some sound against the silence,
against the signs of brightness vanishing.
The railing of the porch dissolves in mist,
the sun has set, and now we're weightless, drifting
as if suspended in the blackening air.
His sphere of light no longer seems as clear.
Maybe he knows the lamplight isn't sunlight.
Maybe he feels he too is disappearing
into the darkness like this porch and chair.
He has to sing, he has to keep on singing,
to know he's really here.

Relic

Here is a bird's breastbone,
the keel of a ship scrubbed clean

of its cargo and rigging, its ribcage
laid bare in this harbor of grasses.

Each morning the sun finds it
and bleaches it into a basket

the snail sleeps in, no longer
robin or finch, but a shelter

for beetles or worms. Now I place it
carefully in the garden

to lie among asters and dahlias
who drink from the sky it fell from

and sing without throats or voices
and flutter and preen without feathers

and fly in the winds of October
and die and go back to the loam.

Ode

Dome of sunlight and leaves,
scatter of birdsong,

the rain starting
and stopping,

and in the shade
of your branches, a gold beam.

I can tell you don't know
what you are doing

though at times you seem to,

fluttering this way
and that

in the light, talking
all morning.

*

I would like to thank you
for your persistence,

the way you begin
a new life every April,

the way you drop
everything in a hurry,

gold, ochre, brown,

[71]

red of pin oaks and maples
fueling the loam.

I've noticed how cold you are
in the white field, shorn of everything,

though of course you don't feel—
forgive me.

I was only thinking
of the long winter
we came through,

someone I love
dying,

and then the leaves
unfurling their many stanzas,

and then the birds.

*

Star-shaped, heart-shaped,
ovals of birch, beech, hornbeam,

pendulous blossoms, white
skittery bells.

I want to say
bole, petiole, umbel

as if you heard me.

There I go again
making you sentient,

making you want things
you wouldn't,

when what I admire
most is your reticence,

how you can be
and not say.

Acknowledgments

Grateful acknowledgment is made to the editors of magazines in which some of these poems first appeared:

AGNI: "Next Summer's Garden," "Winter Move"
Alaska Quarterly Review: "In the Frame"
Atlanta Review: "December: in the South"
Cave Wall: "In the Butterfly Aviary"
Five A.M: "Evening at a Mountain Inn"
The Gettysburg Review: "Apple," "Ode," "Relic"
Harvard Review Online: "After"
The Hudson Review: "All Morning," "Here, in the Piedmont," "Sunflowers"
Missouri Review: "Autumn," "In Tennessee," "Lakewood Path," My Junco," "Sandhill Cranes"
The Sewanee Review: "Auguries," Prognosis," "Sketchbook & Journal," "Steps," "The Spider"
The Southern Review: "From a Park Bench," "In the Clearing," "Lens," "The Missing Girl"
Southwest Review: "February Thaw"
Wisconsin Review: "A Death in Winter"
The Yale Review: "Fall Changes," "Moving South," "Sudden," "The Copperhead"

"Sudden" and "In the Frame" also appeared in the online anthology, *Poetry Daily*. "From a Park Bench," "Lens" and "In the Clearing" were reprinted on the Academy of American Poets' website, *poets.org*.

"From a Park Bench": "Life is the saddest thing there is, next to death" is taken from Edith Wharton's memoir, *A Backward Glance*. The phrase, "one friend like no other," appears in Millicent Bell's *Edith Wharton and Henry James*.

About the Author

Patricia Hooper is the author of four previous books of poetry: *Separate Flights, Other Lives, At the Corner of the Eye,* and *Aristotle's Garden.* She is also the author of a chapbook, *The Flowering Trees,* and four children's books. Her poems have appeared in many magazines, including *The Atlantic Monthly, The American Scholar, Poetry, The Hudson Review, Ploughshares, The Southern Review,* and *The Kenyon Review.* A graduate of the University of Michigan, where she earned B.A. and M.A. degrees, she has been the recipient of The Norma Farber First Book Award of the Poetry Society of America, The Bluestem Award for Poetry, the Anita Claire Scharf Award from the University of Tampa Press, a Writer's Community Residency Award from the National Writer's Voice, the Laurence Goldstein Award for Poetry from *Michigan Quarterly Review,* and the Roanoke-Chowan Award from the North Carolina Literary and Historical Association for *Separate Flights.* She lives in North Carolina.

About the Book

Wild Persistence has been set in Janson Text, a digital font based on matrices originally cut by the Hungarian-Transylvanian priest Miklos Kis (1650-1702) and named in honor of the Dutch printer-publisher Anton Janson, who used the types during the seventeeth century and was believed for many years to have created them. The original matrices survived in the holdings of the Stempel Foundry in Germany, and they were highly valued by D. B. Updike, Stanley Morison, and others concerned with the revival of fine printing. The book was designed and typeset by Richard Mathews at the University of Tampa Press.

Poetry from the University of Tampa Press

Lance Larsen, *What the Body Knows*
Michael Lavers, *After Earth**
Julia B. Levine, *Ask**
Julia B. Levine, *Ditch-tender*
Nancy Chen Long, *Light into Bodies**
Sarah Maclay, *Whore**
Sarah Maclay, *The White Bride*
Sarah Maclay, *Music for the Black Room*
Peter Meinke, *Lines from Neuchâtel*
Peter Meinke, *Tasting Like Gravity*
John Willis Menard, *Lays in Summer Lands*
Kent Shaw, *Calenture**
Barry Silesky, *This Disease*
Eric Smith, *Black Hole Factory**
Jordan Smith, *For Appearances**
Jordan Smith, *The Names of Things Are Leaving*
Jordan Smith, *The Light in the Film*
Lisa M. Steinman, *Carslaw's Sequences*
Lisa M. Steinman, *Absence & Presence*
Marjorie Stelmach, *Bent upon Light*
Marjorie Stelmach, *A History of Disappearance*
Matthew Sumpter, *Public Land*◊
Ira Sukrungruang, *In Thailand It Is Night*◊
Richard Terrill, *Coming Late to Rachmaninoff*
Richard Terrill, *Almost Dark*
Matt Yurdana, *Public Gestures*

* Denotes winner of the Tampa Review Prize for Poetry
◊ Denotes winner of the Anita Claire Scharf Award